For Marilyn T.
—stuck on you—

You're sitting around with nothing to do,
When the doorbell goes *prrring!* Here's a parcel for you—
A mysterious package in paper and string;
You unwrap it to find a most puzzling thing.
But don't become lost in the A-MAZE-ING views—
Just solve all the riddles to work out the clues.
In times of confusion, when nothing is plain,
Stick close to the page and—P.S. Use your brain!

The Right combination to get in the box
Is not "Open, Sesame" or even three knocks.
Four numbers are SENT and Left as a clue.
For the Right way to turn them, it's quite up to you.
Each number will follow the number before—
Add them all up. What's Left? 34!

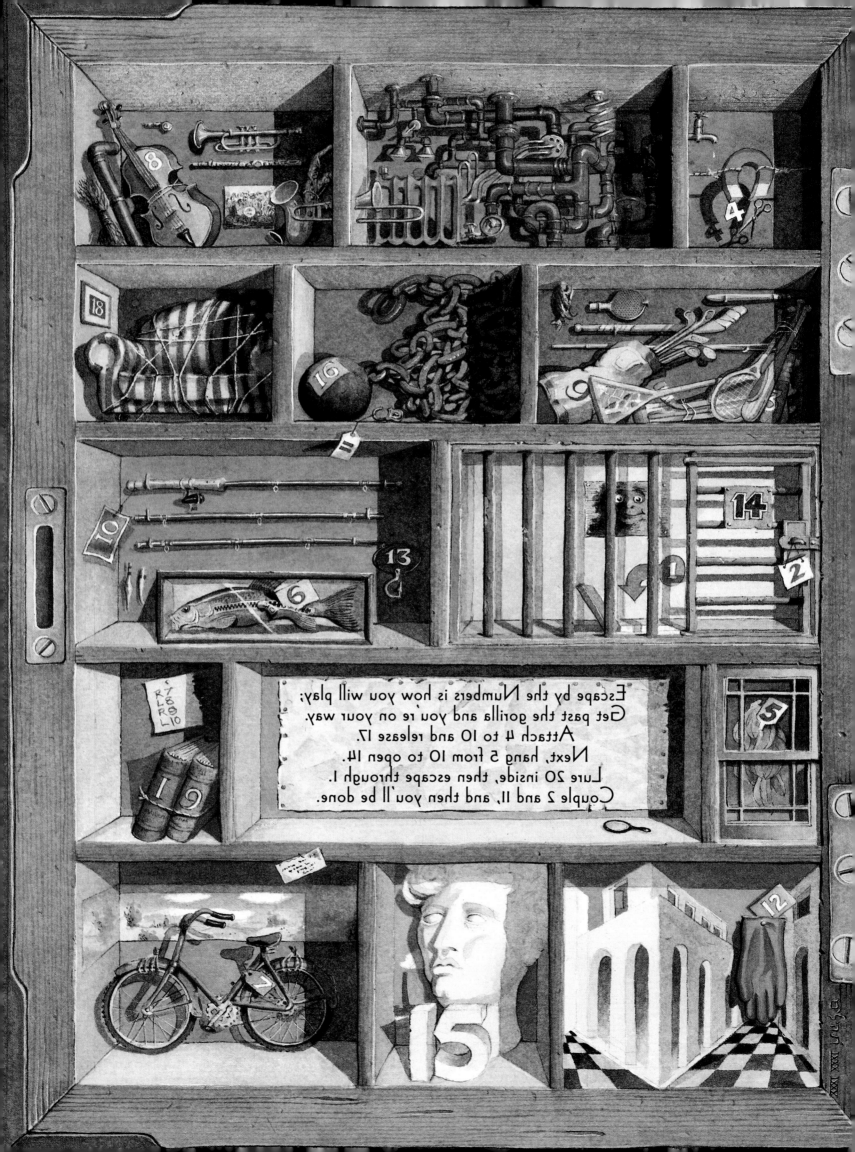

Escape by the Numbers is how you will play;
Get past the gorilla and you're on your way.
Attach 4 to 10 and release 17.
Next, hang 5 from 10 to open 14.
Lure 20 inside, then escape through 1.
Couple 2 and 11, and then you'll be done.

END

START

Escape from this scrape
—you will in a trice—
By using a coin
Or a marker and dice.

Land on a ladder,
Run up, though it's steep.
Land on a puzzle,
Just solve it and leap—

Six whole squares forward,
But—shivers and shakes—
It's all the way back
If you land on the snakes.

The OCEAN TOWER is the trick;
To reach it, you'll do arithmetic.
Be cautious—there are several ways
To make it through this mile-high maze.

Don't stop now to make a fuss—
Or you'll be dinner for an octopus!
If you're CRAFTY, there is no catch
To getting safely down the hatch.
One fits, one twists, one holds up plugs.
One snips, and one red herring tugs.
Go up four times (you've been down five),
And then you might escape alive.

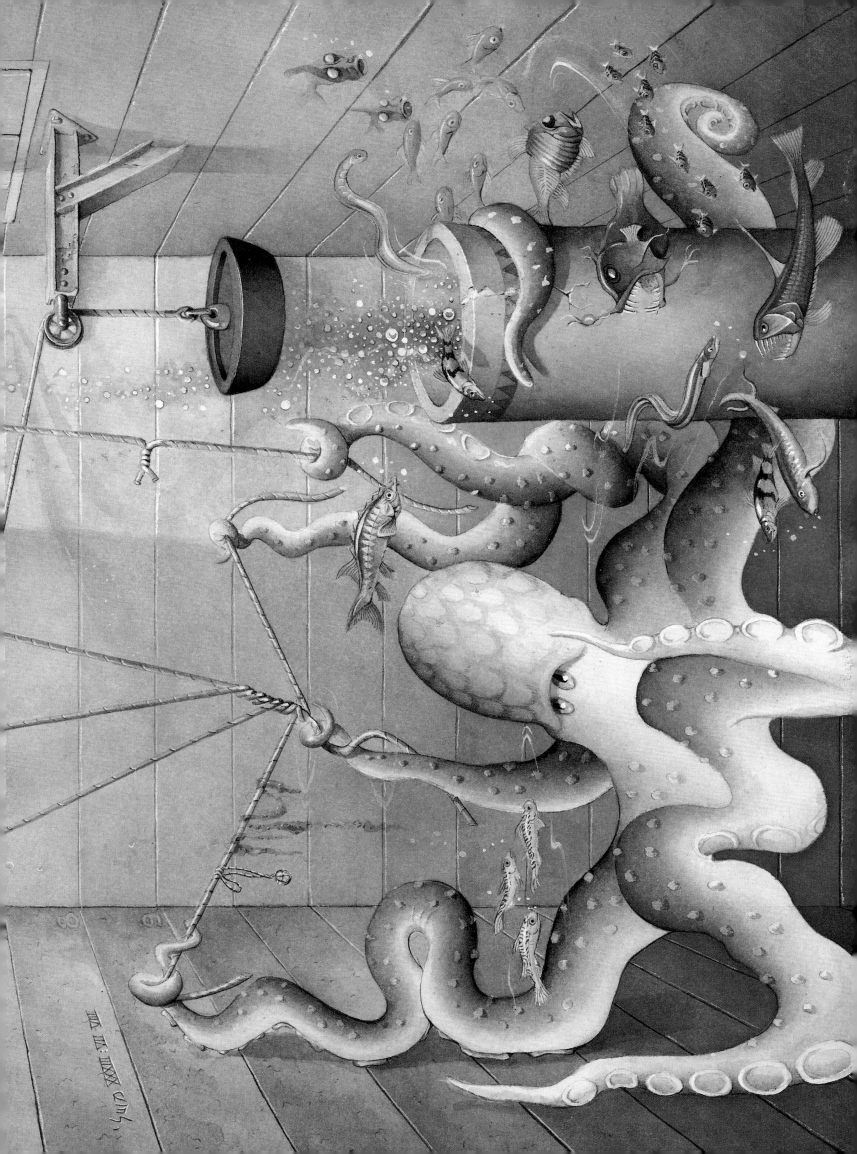

The blocks, you see, a Tower make—
Stack them up to cross the lake.
A jigsaw in a stone disguise
That you'll assemble with your eyes.
But not so fast—don't rush or race—
You must not fit one piece in place
Until you've found and solved for sure
The problem in the piece before.

To clear the stairs, you'll recognize,
The first step is to MAGNETIZE.
But there is an order to contrive:
The balls must finish 1 to 5.
Come from behind and PUSH them down,
Going the long way around.

And as you get them under way,
Beware what else comes into play—
The ratchet works the Dragon's Gate;
One drops you in it if you're late.
So what you need, much more than pluck,
Is speed and timing. Go! Good luck!

15000

15¢

10,000

15000

15¢

1

2

3

3

1 4 5 6

2 4 5 6

And now, at last, a simple game! The highest total is your aim. Use your dice and coin once more to get yourself a MONSTER score. Add up your own points as you go forward and backward with each throw. Get the REPLAY —if you dare. Read the instructions on each square.

OUT

REPLAY

OUT

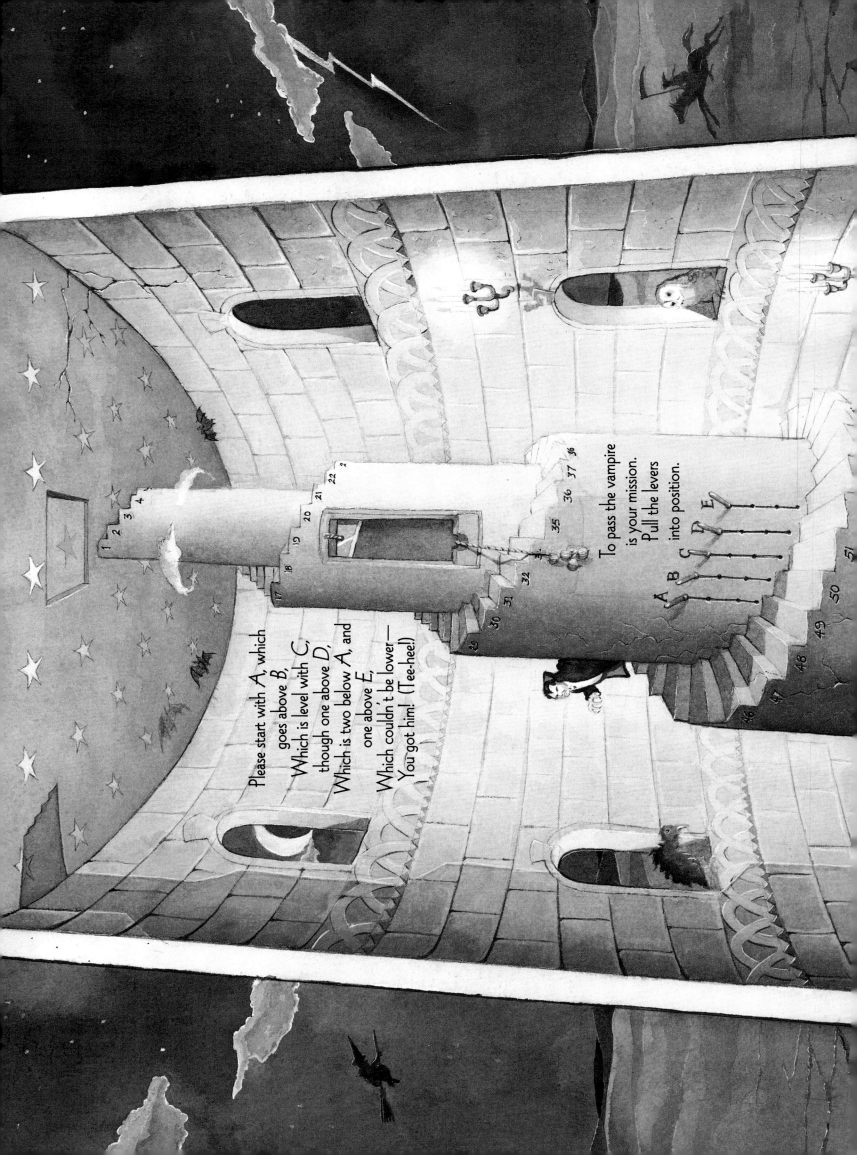

Please start with A, which
goes above B,
Which is level with C,
though one above D,
Which is two below A, and
one above E,
Which couldn't be lower—
You got him! (Tee-hee!)

To pass the vampire
is your mission.
Pull the levers
into position.

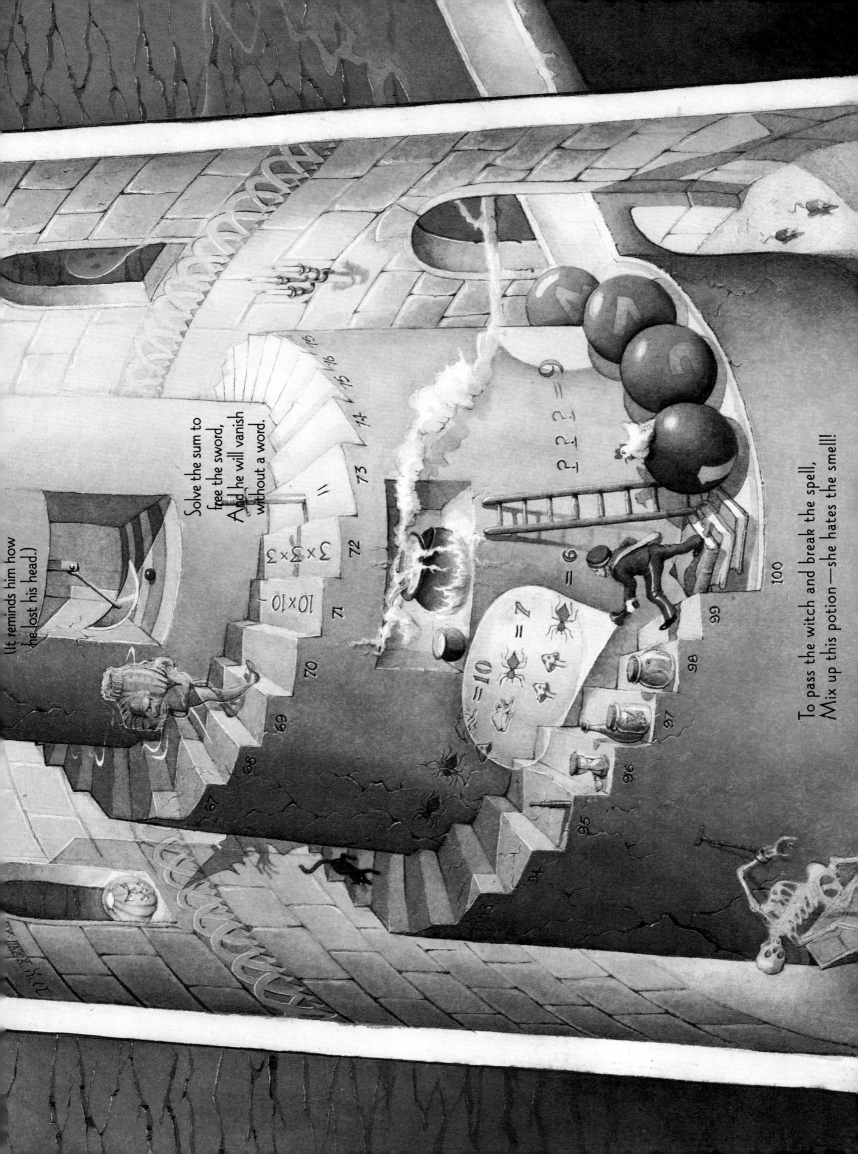

(It reminds him how he lost his head.)

Solve the sum to free the sword,
And he will vanish without a word.

10×10
$3 \times 3 \times 3$
$=$

To pass the witch and break the spell,
Mix up this potion—she hates the smell!

The map room s next,   a sticky trap,
So while the spider takes a nap,
Start at the ladder and navigate
Your way through each coordinate.
Some are false and some are true;
The secret door is webless, too.

At last, the greatest
mystery—
A box within a box?
Maybe.
But here's a question: *When is tea?*
Complete the jigsaw—find the key.

There is no need to feel downhearted
Because you're right back where you started.
To find these things you missed before,
Go back through the box once more!

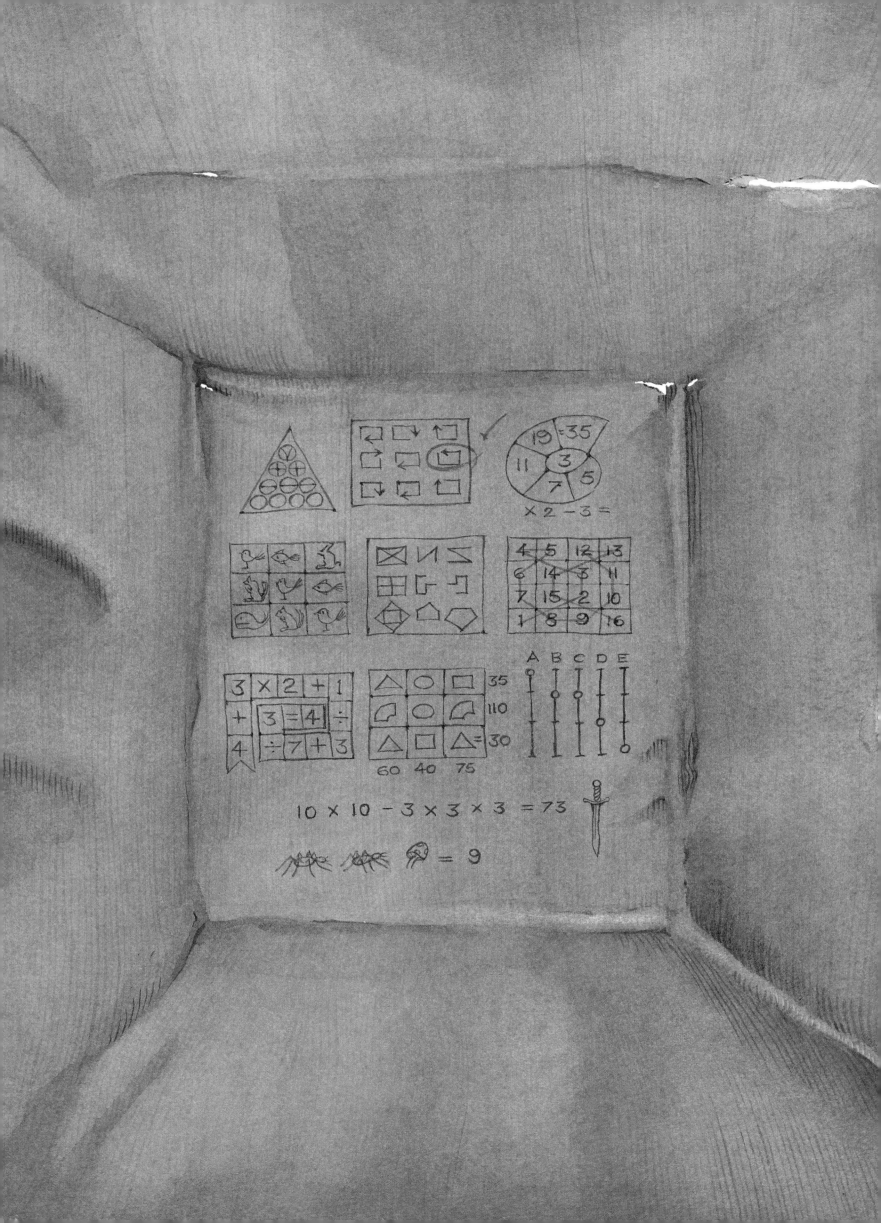

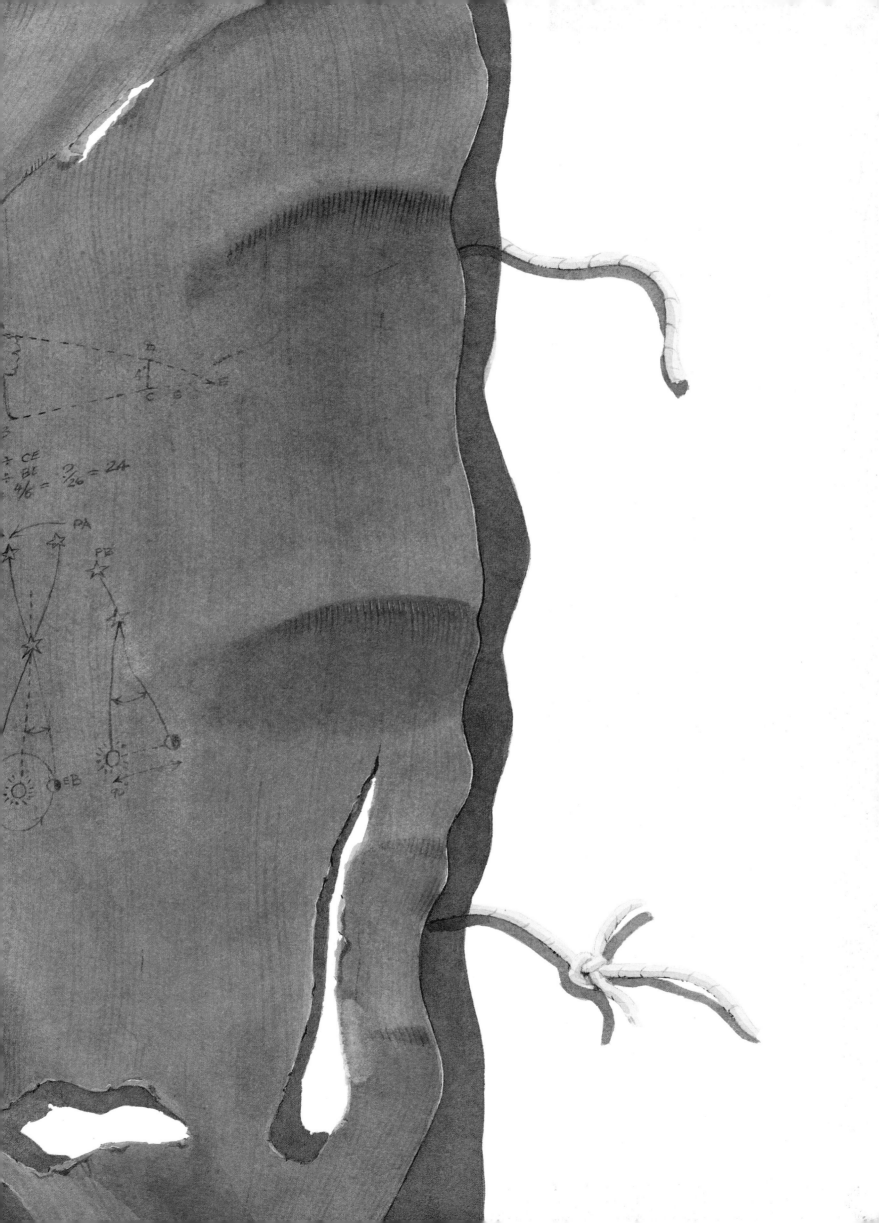

Copyright © 1994 by John Talbot   All rights reserved.

Library of Congress Cataloging-in-Publication Data

Talbot, John, date

It's for you / by John Talbot. — 1st American ed.

p.   cm.

ISBN 0-525-45402-0

1. Picture puzzles — Juvenile literature.   2. Mathematical
recreations — Juvenile literature.   [1. Picture puzzles.
2. Mathematical recreations.]   I. Title.

GV1507.P47T32   1995

793.73 — dc20   94-41236   CIP   AC

First published in the United States in 1995 by Dutton Children's Books,

a division of Penguin Books USA Inc.   375 Hudson Street, New York, New York 10014

Originally published in Great Britain in 1994 by Andersen Press Ltd., London.

Printed in Italy   Typography by Semadar Megged   First American Edition

10 9 8 7 6 5 4 3 2 1